Unimaginable

Losing a Child to the Disease of Addiction

LIZ PETTIT

Soul Bloom Press
www.soulbloompress.com

"Liz Pettit opens her heart as she invites you to take part in her journey of the purest love and the most unthinkable loss... Her unique writing style is poignant, poetic and most importantly, honest... Be prepared to be inspired by her grace and resilience as you take a walk on this path with her."

—DOROTHY DiGILIO,
Certified Family Recovery Specialist and Grief Educator

To all who walk this path of loss and hope.
And to my amazing son and wanderer of the cosmos: Zach.

CONTENTS

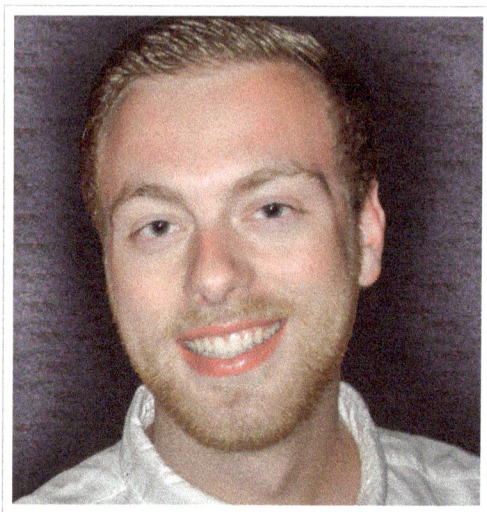

ZACHARY M. PETTIT

April 15, 1994–January 28, 2018

INTRODUCTION

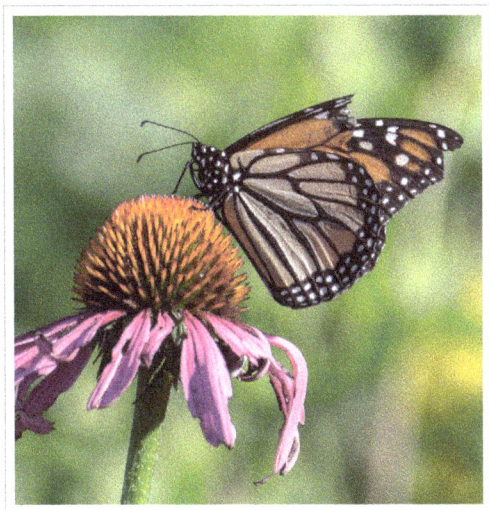

In a sunny meadow I spotted a lone Monarch butterfly. His wings were rather tattered, but somehow he was still keepin' on. It made me think of life and death, and also of how Zach managed for many years with a tattered wing: he kept on until he no longer could. Or rather, until his struggles with substance-use disorder and social anxiety—ultimately the drugs—left him unable to fly any longer.

Early on a January morning in 2018, my heart shattered into a million pieces. I walked into Zach's bedroom to find that he had died in the night.

I never, ever thought this would be Zach.

Walking into his bedroom that winter morning, finding he had departed this life: this was not supposed to be part of the equation of him finding his feet in recovery, of getting relief from his social anxiety. No one wants to be an addict, and Zach tried so hard to maintain his sobriety, but the tools and time weren't enough.

As a parent of a child with substance-use disorder, you try never to let go of hope. I never thought that Zach would be part of the staggering and tragic statistics of accidental drug overdose. The profound mourning that comes with the death of a child can be beyond any other loss in life. It is a journey no parent should ever have to take.

And yet, somehow in this devastating loss, life moves forward, and softens, and becomes not only bearable—but at times joyful. Nature and wildlife, especially birds, have also provided a healing in my heart that I never expected. Support from friends, family, and especially those who also walk this path has been a blessing in finding peace in such an immense loss. That, I am grateful for.

I

LOSS

"Whoever survives a test, whatever it may be,
must tell the story. That is her duty."
—Elie Wiesel

Darkness

1 | 1.28.18

I don't know how sleep will come
On the eve after my son's death.
I lay here, numb, the night light adding
Its faux comfort to an already darkest of nights.

Zach is still here, a few miles away, as his human shell.
I know he is cold, and stiff, and alone.
And in complete darkness,
He sleeps.
There is no other choice now for him
But sleep.

His light is gone.

I hope to dream of him
In a different sleep
Where he's softly snoring
The rise and fall of the covers
As he breathes
As his heart beats
Alive. The glow of life.
I can smile warmly as I see him, and know
He'll awaken that day.

I hope to dream this dream
Every night
For the rest of my life.

Pressed flowers from Zach's Quaker memorial meeting

2 | SATURDAYS

It's always the same, the story.
Saturday.
My birthday lunch with my sister.
Tea and laziness.
Going to pick up Zach at work.
Seeing him walk across the parking lot towards my car.
He is high.
My stomach sinks, my heart races.
It is the worst feeling.

An addict son.

The disgust.

The anger.

We were going to have birthday dinner together.

No.

"What did you take" I say.

"Just an edible" he says.

Lies.

We drive home, he nods off.

All droopy eyed and stoned.

Slurred speech.

I worry, what has he taken, what would happen if I took him to the ER?

He goes to his room. I worry.

He is sleeping with the light on, 7pm.

I wake him, he bumbles down.

Scrounging for food.

I film him with my iPhone.

Last time, I said, "I am going to show you what you look like"

On drugs.

"What, I have a headache is all!" he says.

Lies.

"Do you want to watch a movie" he says.

"No" I say.

I go to bed.

He goes to bed.

7am.

I did not hear him all night.

I make coffee.

Feed the birds.

Go to wake him.
Tap on the door.
Open.
"Zach" I say.
Silence.
I see him, still.
Covered.
Sleeping.
Peaceful.
Gray.
He is dead.

Zach's tiny mittens

3 | FOR ZACH

I came across your tiny
fleece mittens today
tucked back in a sock drawer
somehow, having gone unnoticed for this long

simple and fingerless
flat oval teal pods
I remember them well
such small hands
wriggling around, skin and fleece
together deciding who was softest

I thought of how old these mittens were
today,
23 years old
and how young you were
when you wore them,
7 months young

I slipped two fingers in
to feel what your little hands felt
all those years ago
so cozy
so loved, you were
ours to dote on, our only little boy

I didn't know then
that you'd be gone
23 years later
I didn't know then
that I would never slip
these same mittens
on your own son or daughter's hand
one day

I didn't know a lot of things, then
—anxiety, addiction, depression, death—
and never dreamed I'd only have you
for what feels like
just yesterday
putting mittens on your
1-year old hands.

I DID know, in the end
the constants, the many, many aspects
of who you were
and who you always will be:

My amazing son
overflowing with such
gentle kindness,
a genuine,
radiant heart
full of love to give

Of course, you can still
be that boy, be that man
a mystical energy
untethered
unbound, in a world
I can only dream of,
a life in which I know you,
my beloved son,
are very much now living.

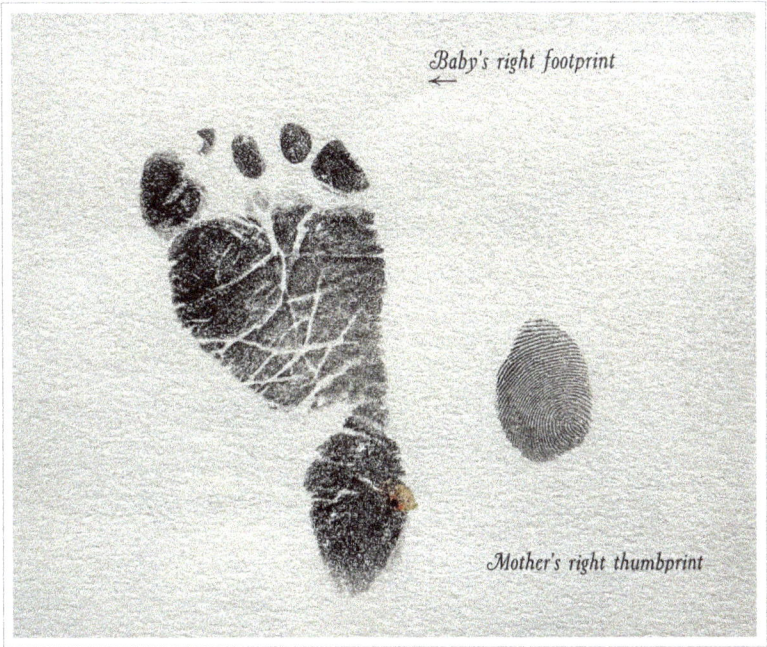

Baby's right footprint

Mother's right thumbprint

4

Your son dies, one day
and there's this odd scattering for the hills
people—friends, relatives
not all
but people who you wouldn't have guessed
had you played a strange game once:
"Hey, if your good friend's kid died, what would you do?"

Could the answer be anything but the obvious?

They tell me "Oh It's not you, it's them."
And I wonder
Of all the times for it to be them,
Why does that have to be now?

Because really, how can it possibly be now?
Perhaps pretend to be someone else
instead of you.

I found Zach's footprints next to my thumbprints
on a fancy hospital birth certificate
I don't recall that memory of the day, my inked print, his tiny feet,
a tiny speck of dried blood
Goodness,
the exhaustion
and exaltation of Zach coming into this world.

And now, this silence.
This distance.
Zach's death echoed into a small niche of nothingness.
It's another layer of grief
that oughtn't be.

One of Zach's favorite places

5 | GUILT

There is a different kind of guilt that comes
when your child dies.
And you are the parent, the always caretaker,
no different than when they were babies or toddlers or teens.

They are always yours to care for, always.

Yet here, I didn't do what a mom is supposed to do.
Here,
a short hallway, footsteps away
a telling silence that only a mom
would ever know.

But I did not know.

I did not know.

I don't know if I ever can convey
the meaning of the word
Guilt
in my new world, now,
Zach dying as I slept.

As I slept.
and had morning coffee.
and fed the birds.

My boy, my boy.
I am so, so sorry you are gone...

Zach and the merry go round

6

Today I received the follow-up call from the detective about Zach's case. He had reached out to me late last fall, almost two years now after Zach's death. He told me that the forensic unit had the capability of extracting data from a locked iPhone. Since Zach's heroin was lethal, the person who sold it to Zach could be charged with "felony drug delivery resulting in death."

Umph. Even writing that is a punch to the gut.

The detective shared details about text messages, specifically those that could be helpful to the case. These were difficult to hear. Some facts really should just stay in a file in a drawer somewhere, for moms not to have to know, especially given that in the end none was incriminating enough to pursue anything further.

I never had the emotional energy to get riled up about Zach's dealer being caught. It didn't change anything. Zach would still be dead. Some young misguided person would go to jail—deservedly so, yet changing nothing. This would never bring my boy back.

Now, they will be closing Zach's case.

It's difficult in this instance to be drawn back into the days surrounding Zach's death, as those memories are fraught with dread and pain. I mean, sometimes replaying things is therapeutic, and I don't ever want to forget when Zach left us.

It's complicated, isn't it?

I didn't expect this wave of sadness to fill me like it did today. The fresh reminder of Zach being gone. And another sad chapter closing.

Zach's bedroom, a hang-out for Luna when she naps, and me, when I journal.
Zach departed this life from here.

7

I think about the moments when I walked into Zach's bedroom that morning. It was just him and me. I wonder sometimes, was this moment similar to people who have had near-death experiences, who've 'died' and come back? The moment where the spirit/ soul leaves one's body but is still here? I wonder if Zach was, in that spirit-y way, still here. Shrouding me with as much love as he could give. I find it fascinating to ponder this, even though the actual moment was and will be the worst—absolutely unparalleled worst— moment of my life.

When I moved, I gave Zach's bed—this sacred place of his death—to a local charity. His bed was a hangout for me and Luna for some time after he died, super comforting in sensing him, even though, yes, he died right there.

The first time I sat, and then lay, in that place, the tears spilled oh so easily. How could they not?

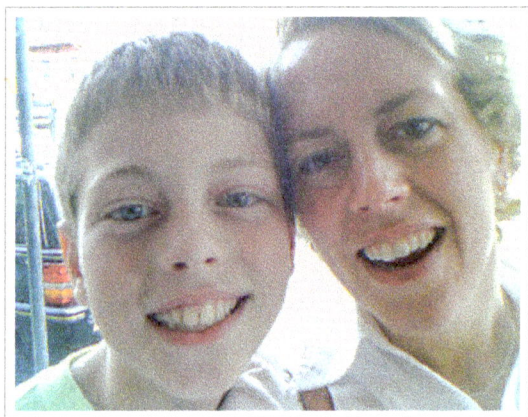

First cellphone selfie, Zach and me, 2006

8

There is no depth to the despair of your child's dying.

There is no depth to the pain in my heart, knowing Zach's story of living with substance-use disorder and anxiety. The loss for the parent of a child, for any reason, is unbearable. All come with their own nightmares of loss.

Zach's story comes with the bonus of the disease leading to his death: the many aspects that were so incredibly difficult for him, and then for those who loved him. Those pieces, those aspects, can be really ugly. The painful memories. Were Zach alive, he'd have his own lengthy tales to tell. I only know of some of them, most likely. Thank God for that.

Zach needed money to buy drugs. He worked many jobs, and in the end, almost everything went to support his drug habit. This is not shocking, of course. Selling my camera and iPad without telling me: also not too startling in the world of drug addicts.

The guilt and shame that comes with just this facet of substance-use disorder is huge. I am heartbroken that Zach had to live with the guilt and shame of what this shitty disease did to his life.

There is a movie called *Ben is Back*, starring Julia Roberts, where Ben is her son struggling with addiction and recovery. It happened to come out in 2018, the year Zach died, though I didn't watch it until maybe the following year. Without seeing it, you wouldn't fully get the sense or full context: the scene that floored me was quite daring, though clearly common enough to be included.

In *Ben is Back*, at one point in the story Ben's family dog is taken, and Ben goes with his mom to try to find it. He thinks the dog was taken by someone linked to his addict life. He and his mom pull up at a house—it's nighttime, Ben goes to the door, an older man answers, he and Ben talk, Ben comes back to the car. His mom asks him what it was about, pushes for an explanation. He tells his mom, "You don't want to know. Some things you just don't want to know."

I know what that thing is. It is a thing that, as Zach's mom, I could curl up in a ball and weep about for days: Zach had to sell his body for drug money. I feel no shame around this, simply a profound, deep sorrow. My heart aches and aches that this wonderful, amazing young man had to do this. I want to scoop Zach up, hold him tight, take away all of the pain, and heal a life that was a jumbled, hopeless mess in the end.

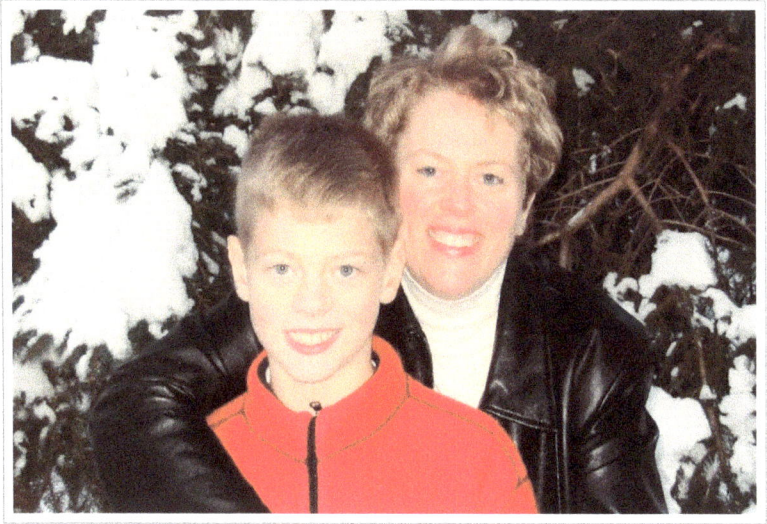

Christmastime, 2005

9

Tough love.

Man, what a crappy concept. An oxymoron. Love is love: there's nothing that should be tough about it.

One month before Zach died, we gave him the ultimatum that he'd have to move out, to figure things out by himself. See, he had started using drugs again. We'd told him that one more strike was it.

Tough love. Zach is a poster child for how this concept doesn't work. He texted me a few days after we told him, saying "Mom, what am I gonna do?" Soul crushing, those words. My heart still aches when I think about that.

This illustrates why the disease of addiction is so much bigger than just the person with the addiction. As Zach's mom, I tried desperately to do what I could to help him find the answers he needed. There's no parenting manual here, no self-help book.

Imagine, piling even more onto someone who's already struggling and desperate. It's sad and broken this concept of tough love, to someone as vulnerable as Zach—so desperate for sobriety, so smothered by his anxiety, and most likely depression too.

One of the most difficult things I had to do as a mom was to parent Zach, the addict. Love in those dark moments of Zach's active addiction was a tall order. Yet, if I could scream one thing from a mountaintop now, it's to *love* your child, the best you can, unconditionally.

Just, love.

10

It didn't hit me until perhaps a few weeks after Zach passed: he was an organ donor. By the time I found him, hours gone, it seemed that none of him could be donated.

It's another sad, shitty chapter in this awful story.

Today, on the anniversary of his departure from this life, I cried bitter tears at that fact. Imagine if someone could have seen through the eyes that Zach saw the world through! Even greater, if someone could have had his beating heart.

Zach's heart!

Zach at Above & Beyond concert, TLA Philadelphia, February 2012

II
FINDING MY WAY

"It may be that some little root of the sacred tree still lives.
Nourish it then, that it may leaf and bloom and fill with singing birds."
—*Black Elk*

Thanksgiving Day, 2 months before Zach's death

11

Today is International Overdose Awareness Day.

I will always celebrate Zach an infinite number of joyful times via photos and stories. It's also important to recognize and talk about the struggles and pain that led to him leaving us way, way too soon.

This photo is from his last Thanksgiving. I think it encapsulates where Zach was at that moment. Zach's social anxiety was pronounced and debilitating for him, a silent torment that he hid well. Many people thought he was just quiet.

Zach spent years and much frustration in trying to find relief in treatment, through psychiatrists, therapy, and meds. Ultimately, medicine failed him. This is a fact that each and every clinician who treated him agreed with, when I shared the ridiculously sad news of his overdose. It was not a matter of blame, but a matter of how little we know about the brain, and substance-use disorder, and the complicated meshing of treating both successfully. How tragic it is that based on those factors, Zach is now gone from this human life.

And so, while I have no idea what this place is that they call the afterlife, I like to think—I truly believe—that he shed that chronic demon of anxiety and addiction fully the moment he turned into a beautiful ball of cosmic energy, and split this popsicle stand for a much, much better place.

And that—that, my friends—makes looking at this photo oh so much easier.

Miss you, my sweet beautiful Zach.

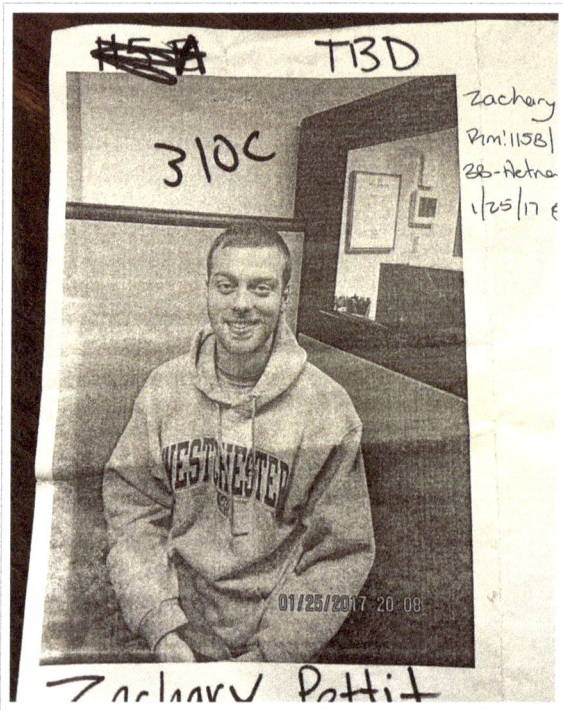

Zach entering recovery, January 2017

12

I'm moving in a month. I've been organizing and going through things: tossing, packing, giving to charity.

This past weekend we went through all of Zach's childhood boxed items. There was some fantastic school/artwork from his time at the local Friends school. We spent several hours, smiling, pausing, so many emotions, basically poignant and fun and sad: all of it, as you could imagine. Lots of keepers in the mix.

Last night, I came across a piece of my luggage that had a piece of duct tape with Zach's name on it. I realized it was what he used when he went to rehab a year prior to his death. I went through to make sure it was fully cleaned out, and in the front zip pocket, found paperwork. The top page was a printer-quality grainy black and white photo of him, the evening he was admitted to the rehab facility. The photocopy was half wrinkled and folded, with sharpie marker indicating his room, and the timestamp of his intake.

Here I am looking at this pic of Zach, loopy on Xanax, smiling for the camera as he sat on a chair during intake. I have both love and hate for this photo. Love for this as cute and comical, mostly because of the context of this as a positive juncture in his life. Love for finding this photo: newly-discovered photos are gold. Hate for the reminder of what drugs turned him into when he used. I'd almost always know when Zach had taken drugs by looking at his face, a subsequent knot cinching up in my stomach. The dichotomy of feelings that come from a loved yet addict son stays, even now. Though love always wins.

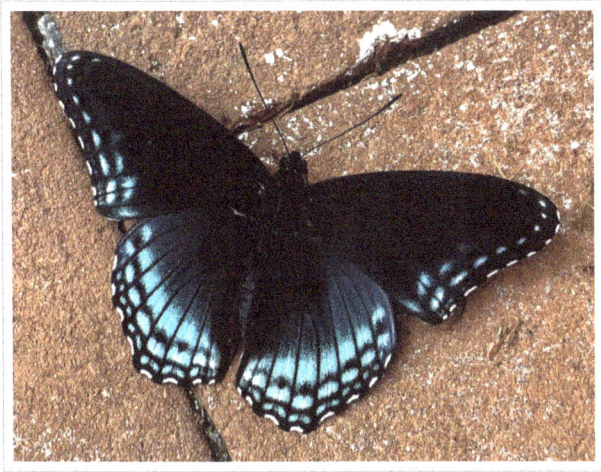

iPhone snap of the Red-spotted Purple Butterfly

13

I went to my therapist appointment with many thoughts from the couple of days prior in tow. It was a somewhat intense session, and not only from the packing and going through all sorts of memories.

In the past few weeks, things have been surfacing from the difficult times when Zach was using. Things that at the time I just couldn't deal with and swept under the rug. But as it goes in life, anything we sweep under the rug—well, it doesn't go away. Even though Zach is now gone. It will stay a big lump under your feet until you lift the rug, sweep it back out, and do something with it. When I saw my therapist, we started to do just that. It was intense. And helpful, to begin the lumpy rug clean up.

When I came out, I was immediately circled by a butterfly flying around maybe ten feet from me, low and to the ground. I got out my iPhone to video him. And then he flew closer and lit on the ground a mere couple feet in front of me. He was beautiful, and one like I'd never seen before. I took photos, and video; moved within inches of him as he sat rather unfazed on the brick sidewalk, slowly moving his wings. I am guessing he'd just emerged recently, and was finding his wings, so to speak. Funny thing about Zach—I mean this butterfly—showing up like he did. Besides being helpful and needed in that moment, it also makes me less a skeptic of signs. You must admit, it's cool having the presence of Zach while struggling on this bumpy path of life without him.

Handsome cap and gown Zach, June 2013

14

Today, in spirit, and with 105 credit hours bundled up in his energy somewhere in the vast universe, Zach will be with 933 undergrads at his University's winter commencement ceremony. He would be walking—10am sharp—with his bachelor's in Computer Science diploma firmly and proudly in hand.

Goodness, imagine that. It is a wonderful and yet incredibly bitter-sweet thought and image to have at the moment.

Of course, I don't know the path that would have been ahead for Zach, had he not overdosed. But in theory, in plan, Zach's 5½ years in college would have finally brought him to a very proud achievement. I like to think he'd have found his feet and been here for this, and oh so much more.

And so this morning, our tall, handsome boy Zach would be in a black cap and gown, with a purple and gold stole and tassel. Picture that, like the photo here from his high school graduation—and then add an even bigger Zach smile. He so should be in that mix of graduates today, beaming. This much I know.

I will celebrate him, and keep the day in my mind, for sure.

Caps off to you, sweet Zach.

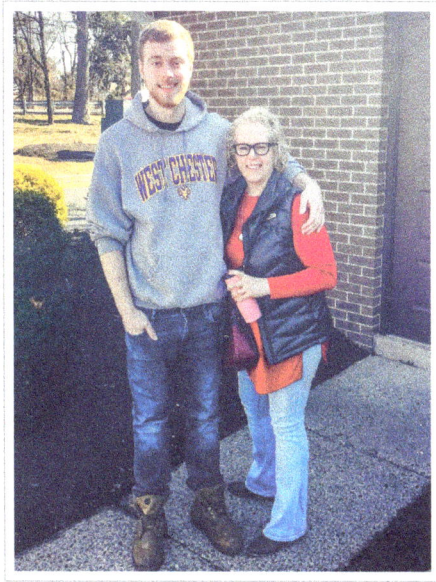

Visiting Zach at the recovery house, a hopeful time. February 2017

15

I remember this day. It feels like the proverbial yesterday: visiting Zach at the recovery house, just a year before he departed this life.

At the time, as a first-time parent of a child in rehab, you're like "You got this Zach! A new life, no drugs, you can get on with your life!" As a mom, I told myself this, nervously chanted it, hoped, worried, hoped some more. Seeing Zach sober helped me to feel positive most of the time. And yet, the slightest bit of "what if" crept in, along with the eventual complete dread at times of "Holy shit—what if this doesn't work?"

And yet you just hope. I hoped. Zach is different, he'll do this, I told myself. He'll find sobriety.

Zach spent a total of seven weeks in a combination of medical rehab and a recovery house, both lacking in tools and time. Insurance dictates the maximum stay and treatment, some magical number that clearly was not enough to set someone like Zach up for success.

Here is a young man, his brain fully altered from drugs—science tells us this—who was still plagued with very active social anxiety, and who was expected to get his act together after a mere seven weeks. It's tragic that this most likely played a role in Zach's death.

After the thirty-five days in the recovery house, Zach was wished well and given paperwork on finding local meetings of NA (Narcotics Anonymous, sibling of Alcoholics Anonymous). There he would need to find his own sponsor. To think that the logic of NA is for Zach, a young man vulnerable and still riddled with social anxiety, to simply up and ask someone to be his NA sponsor. Instead, a much better, caring process could be a sponsor reaching out and saying "Zach, I'd love to help you; let's chat, see how we can do this together." In life, people who need help don't always ask for it. This process added risk to Zach's sobriety, and ultimately to his life. While AA/NA programs work for many in recovery, they do not work for all. I don't believe they worked for Zach.

Zach stepped back out into this world, pushed with only one solution to remain sober. As his mom, I was standing there, uncertain:

"Well, this is what they say to do, so I guess this is it!" I felt blindsided with being handed back my kid.

What if the better fit for Zach was a pharmacological treatment? An alternative holistic, integrative path to sobriety? I did not know of other treatments for Zach back then. In the end, a different path may have led to a different ending. One where Zach was still alive.

But now Zach, my sweet boy, is gone.

I really love this photo of us together.

16

Zach didn't keep much on his night table. This sat propped up, still. It's a card I gave him on his last birthday, more than nine months earlier.

We both loved Narnia. I can now know that he is in that dream, the pain from his anxiety and addiction long, long gone.

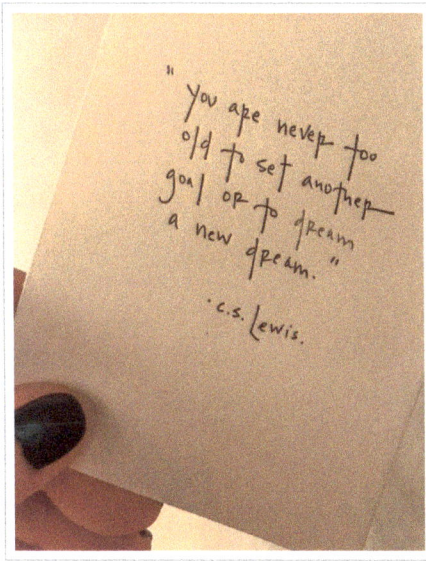

Zach and me at the zoo, 1996

17

I was remembering when Zach was a toddler and little boy. He'd wake up in the wee hours of morning, tiptoe in, and climb into bed with us. Everyone would then fall back to sleep, a good solid, sleepy snuggle. The warmth and soft breath from him, so sweet. Such love.

The other morning in yoga, during shavasana and singing bowls, I had this sense and imagery of climbing into bed with Zach and hugging him, after I found him dead. I wish I had found him sooner, when he was still warm, and soft. I would have just laid there quietly with him, in that early morning hour, peacefully.

Does this seem unimaginable? I hope it does. Until you step into those shoes, you cannot really imagine what you'd do, finding your child dead.

As I lay there myself in this yoga corpse pose, so relaxed, I contemplated what I could not change. That moment of walking into his bedroom. Zach as a child. Now as an adult. No beating heart and soft breath, even more reason to cling to that sweet child. To have stroked his skin, studied every aspect of his beautiful face, held his hand. Hugged him, knowing this was it; soon he would be physically gone, until I was ready to let go forever.

If only time could stand still; if only we could go back. Even if just to that day, even to when the life had gone from him.

This. This is what it's like to lose your child.

Snow Angel Zach

18

I find it oddly comforting remembering the events around Zach's death. But truly, does any of it make sense: what does, or doesn't, comfort vs. terrify us? Tragically sad and devastating, yet import-ant; a validation of so much. Remembering this worst possible nightmare... Yet I never want to forget. Ever.

I thought about that evening, only hours before Zach would die in his sleep. It's only a little part of the story that I replayed, driving home from the grocery store the other day. Have you ever noticed how, when driving alone, the brain really taps into all sorts of emo-tional memories?

So that night, the last one Zach was alive. January 27th, 2018. Zach was as high as a kite. I was disgusted with him. Worried. Living with an addict when they've used drugs brings with it a "what-did-my-kid-take?" fear and worry.

Logically I knew that it was the addiction and the drugs that I hated, a poison to his body, his mind, his life. But man, it's so hard, if not impossible, to separate the two, when your son stands in front of you, all droopy-eyed and slurring and awful. Those were the worst moments in parenting, aside from Zach's actual death.

And that evening I did something that I said I'd do: I got out my iPhone and I took a video of him. Zach fumbling around the kitchen for food, denying that he had used. I had told him the last time he'd used drugs that I would video him the next time, so he could see for himself. And I did.

Six hours later, he would be dead.

The next morning: It was after the dust had settled, the coroner had left, Zach in a black body bag, that I remembered it

The video.

Gil was there: I told him about it. We both knew there was no way we could watch it. I deleted it.

I still think about that, though, to this day.

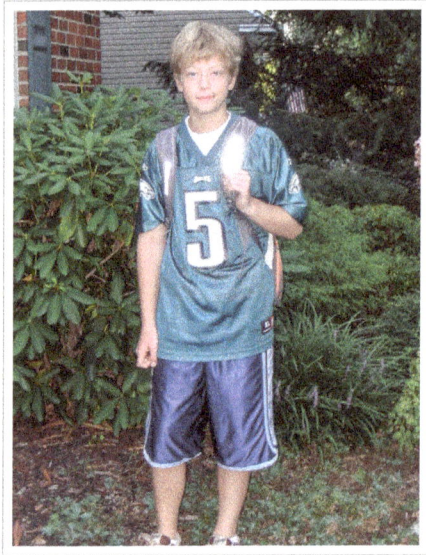

Zach's first day of school, 5th grade

19

Today is sixteen months later. Time after death railroads by: this is a sad fact.

Lucky for me, though: here is an unearthed and ridiculously cute pic of Zach. The one I was missing, of all the thirteen years of first day of school pics.

And while there seems to be a crescendo that builds in replaying the days around Zach's death, so many good memories sway that pendulum away from the heartbreaking trauma that comes from that day. Frankly, I'm amazed that my life has found this space of peace and calm. The brain and heart heal just a bit, somehow.

Having to pack, as laborious as that is, meant stirring up those good memories in going through many boxes and totes that I'd not really looked at since Zach's childhood. Every last piece of artwork, schoolwork, and fun stuff tucked away made for several hours of savoring the treasures of who Zach is. We honored every bit of it: most went into the permanent-keeper pile, and some into the recycling bin.

The photos too. Photos of which I had some recall but were still such a treat to find and revisit. New things of and about Zach that are gently brushed against my heart. I hope I never run out of those moments.

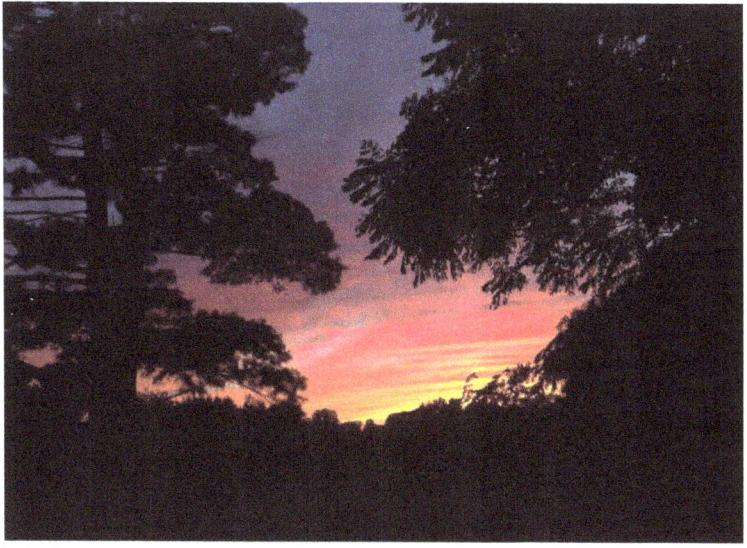

20

I was walking the other evening around my neighborhood. The sky was so pretty, and I made a point to look upwards, as from within my home I don't really have much of a view of sunrise or sunset. I watched the clouds changing as dusk approached, just a hint of pinky-orange gradually growing to that 'sunset clouds' look. Pretty.

As I walked, I thought about Zach, as I do many times during the day. Earlier I saw an ambulance in front of a home nearby: never a good thing to see an ambulance. It reminded me of that time, that dreaded day. Though I guess it was a police car and then the coroner's van the day Zach died; I never did see. No ambulance for

Zach. You don't need EMT or ambulance when there's no hope of life. When you're dead. As I walked beneath more beautiful sky, my thoughts continued with that morning, Zach being taken out of the house in a body bag.

Ok, it's not a cheerful thought, this we know. But I was thinking, reflectively, that maybe only two hours after the medical examiner came, I was already in shock, a zombie, a spectator to someone else's insane tragedy. How on earth did I even let them leave the house? How many people scream hysterically, clinging to the gurney, the body bag (the body!)? How many who've lost their child, literally refuse to let go? I wonder about that.

And then I was thinking: why on earth is it a black bag, of all colors? Why not fluorescent green, or an ocean design with sea turtles, or the sky that I was actually looking at, in that moment? Bring out swatches right then and there when your child is about to be zipped up and taken away. Why a drab, sad, black sack?

So, just some random thoughts. I snapped this picture when all was said and done. Thank goodness for skies like this, right?

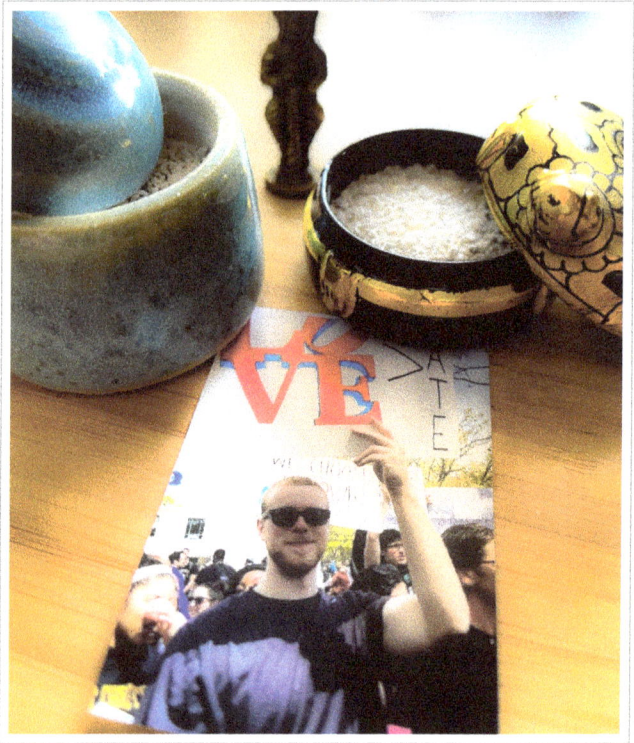

Some of Zach's cremains, in a small handmade pottery urn
and a gold leaf turtle urn

21

It's no surprise that Zach's cremated remains are beautiful. The topic has at times been on my mind, a year today since Zach's cremation.

I wasn't there for Zach's cremation. And I sure wish I could have been, but at the time of being a walking zombie, I suppose it never crossed my mind to ask. Was this even an option, I wondered?

Zach was cremated just two days after his death, though at that moment two days felt like weeks; those early days were ones living in a dark bubble, with no logic of time. Some time later, I happened to find a nifty video describing the entire procedure of cremation, and in processing it in my mind, I grew angry that no options were given surrounding this highly sacred process. The light bulb switched on: "Hey wait a minute, why didn't anyone tell me??"

What I have discovered, in this mess of a child's dying, is that overall people kinda suck with death: people, as those here in this country, in my community, who are the experts, the ones who do this death stuff. Those who are there to say, "Hey Liz, this is how it rolls with your son's dying. Let me tell you all your options, down to the minutest detail, in honoring your dead son."

Consider this: Zach's spirit, his soul, was released from his body at that exact moment of cremation. Is there anything more sacred?

Perhaps it's a guarded assumption or societal norm that I would be horrified at the prospect of being present at Zach's cremation. Loved ones, by default, should be given the option to be present during the actual cremation. Not to see the body burn necessarily, but to be near and know the exact moment of the release of their loved one's—Zach's—soul.

As to the video, it helped me a bit in coming to terms with not being able to change any of the outcomes. I wept bitterly when they stated, "All organic matter is consumed."

A powerful visual, the burning of Zach's body.

I found a journal entry with a great memory surrounding Zach's cremation: The Philadelphia Eagles had just won the football playoffs and were heading to the Superbowl that Sunday after Zach's death. I had written a text to a friend saying "Zach will be cremated tomorrow morning, we have him in his new Eagles jersey and championship tee, jeans, Vans sneakers, and his American eagle purple boxer briefs. Purple!"

So funny, poignant, and bittersweet, I smile every time I remember this.

A Happy Day of your release, Zach. May you wander the infinite possibilities of the cosmos in glory. You are ever so missed.

Zach

22 | REMEMBERING ZACH...

"What is life? It is the flash of a firefly in the night. It is the breath of a buffalo in the wintertime. It is the little shadow which runs across the grass and loses itself in the sunset."
—Crowfoot, Blackfoot First Nation

Today somehow is three years since Zach departed this life, released from the bonds of his anxiety and substance-use disorders. It is a tragedy in which no words can describe the sense of loss of the unassuming, kind, and gentle person Zach was/is.

And yet, life moves forward and somehow things soften, and become not only bearable but, much of the time, joyful. That is what happens when you open your mind and heart to a different relationship with your child—when you welcome in the possibility of signs and presence in wildlife and nature, things that perhaps you hadn't noticed before.

Crowfoot's words on life are blended with that which is beyond this life, I believe. Zach is in the distant call of a Great Horned Owl in the forest at dusk, the symmetrical ripple in turquoise waters from a sea turtle diving below, and always, always, "the little shadow which runs across the grass and loses itself in the sunset." So today we remember Zach, as I do every day, in these photos and with song. It is through these memories we can keep him forever alive in our hearts and minds.

Eastern Pondhawk dragonfly

23

I have two essential-oil diffusers, one in my living area and one in Zach's room. I usually run them both during the day: each has a timer, and there is also a band of light around the base, of which you can click thru and choose one of many variations of colors. Yesterday, I stopped on a sort of fluorescent green in Zach's room, which as it turns out is not a favorite color of mine. I then proceeded to be vexed with the question, "Did Zach like the color green?" I honestly didn't know. And that annoyed me, which is something that happens from time to time, as I can't exactly shout out to him in the other room and ask him.

So, I left it as green.

Today at a local garden, lo and behold, I came upon a fluorescent green dragonfly, the female Eastern Pondhawk, a dragonfly I've never seen before.

Thanks Zach, now I know! Green!

Birds I've met and photographed

24

It's always a gift to see Zach in nature, in a myriad of ways.

Here, it's among the many birds I see. I like to think given what a mystery it is—this afterlife bit—that somehow Zach's being and soul is out there in a way we can't comprehend. That is, until we look at beauties like these.

How can it not be Zach, the way they look at me?

III

LOVE NEVER LEAVES

"The soft bonds of love are indifferent to life and death. They hold through time so that yesterday's love is part of today's and the confidence in tomorrow's love is also part of today's. And when one dies, the memory lives in the other, and is warm and breathing."

—Isaac Asimov

25

"Hey Mom."

"Hey Zach."

I can play this a million times in my head.

San Francisco, Summer of 2014

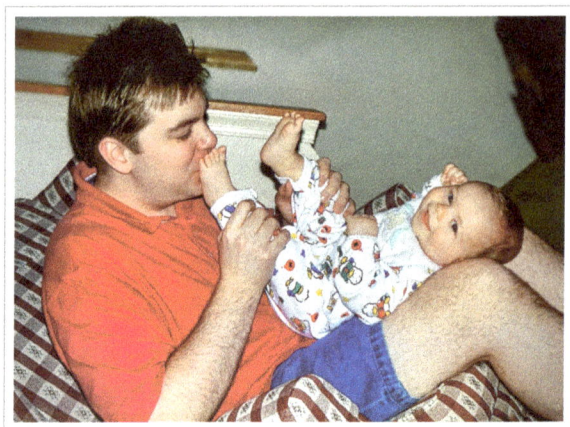

26

There was a time, many years back, when I lamented my marriage ending, but I always thought, "Well, it wasn't all for nothing: I have Zach". . . and then, that piece too shattered, horribly.

I won't say that notion stuck fully: that his loss negated all. Because the things that always existed for Gil and me after our divorce, and then after Zach's death, were our friendship, our decent co-parenting, and of course our profound love for Zach. Zach will always be the source of love in our hearts, both together and apart.

Today, I can find my heart filled with joy and gratitude for Zach having had a Dad who so loved him. And, loves him. He was and is an amazing Dad. Married or not, Gil and I have, and always will share, that special bond of having a child together. Loving Zach through his time on this earth, and now death, and mourning that tragic loss of him, gives Gil and me an experience that no one else can ever share.

Thanks for being a wonderful Dad and friend, Gil. I'm guessing that Zach, in his own special cosmic way, spreads the word about you.

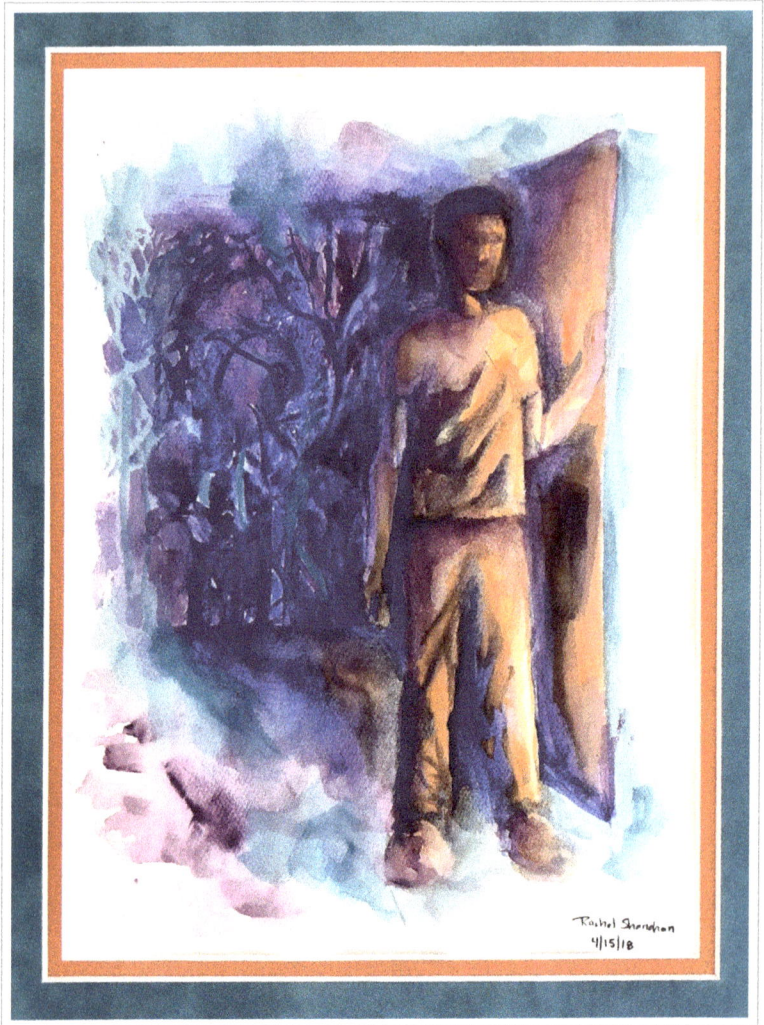

Zach in the Doorway

27

Sometimes in life we have friends who leave one speechless with their kindness, love, and overflowing heart. If that friend happens to be an amazing artist, it can mean being gifted something incredibly special. On Zach's birthday, my friend Rachel surprised me with a watercolor painting she had done, just the day before.

Zach in the Doorway is something that came to Rachel after I told her about a dream I'd had. Zach died in his bedroom with the door closed. Not long after, I dreamt of him opening his bedroom door and walking out. I woke up, the dream feeling very real, as though I'd actually watched it happen at that exact moment. It was a very powerful dream. Rachel's painting is a beautifully interpretive watercolor showing Zach walking out of his bedroom doorway. I love these colors, the deep blue and purple behind Zach, his earthly life behind him, bright and dark both... And then the orange glow radiating out of—or into—his new other-worldly life.

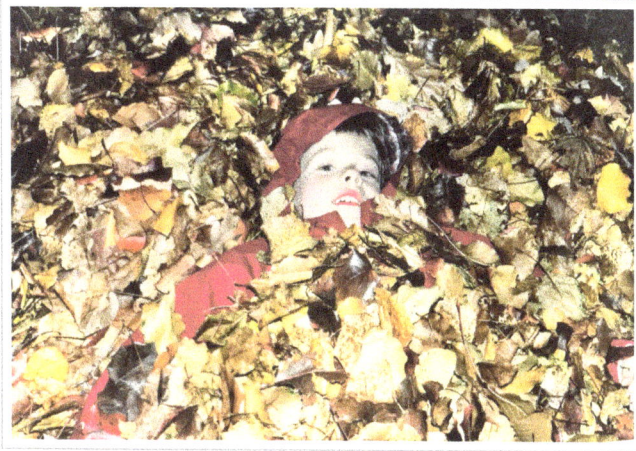

28

In so many ways I wish I didn't know any of my newish lovely friends who also walk this path. Yes, I'd forsake all of them and magically go back a year ago.

A year ago, where I can imagine Zach walking in the front door, maybe while I'm in the kitchen making dinner. I can hear his voice, always. "Hey Mom," sight unseen.

And he would be my son, in that moment of time. Alive.

And I would always say back "Hey Zach."

It doesn't sound like much, but it was the minimalist language we had between us at times. It's enough to make me close my eyes and imagine hearing him, feeling his presence. I can smile.

Tonight, I drove to Valley Forge Park. I watched yet another stunning sunset, the 251st since Zach decided to get a closer look at that big ol' sun. I thought about earlier that day, having Zach there in spirit, as both my newish and old friends showed up at a 5K fundraiser event for Zach and other young people who too lost their lives. These friends—"warrior" moms and dads who also lost a child to this disease—warm my heart and also make me yearn for a different outcome. It's just the way it goes.

You are loved, Zach, by many. This is a fact that will never, ever change.

I wonder how awesome cool that reddish-orange excellent sunset looks up close, Zach. You'll have to tell me one of these days.

Stargazing at Joshua Tree National Park, June 2018

29

"So unassuming and gentle" is a short but succinct quote my sister used when describing Zach. And, my word, that pretty much is him in a nutshell.

Today is Zach's 3 ½ year angelversary.

That's a fun word some of my friends use, even though the text-book 'angel' reference—halos, wings, bright light radiating from what is their celestial yet same earthly look—isn't the same as I imagine it to be.

I imagine Zach as little flecks of magnificent cosmic energy, all carrying the beauty and love of who he is. All those super cool images of different parts of galaxies taken by the fancy Hubbell space telescope, Zach's clearly in there, somewhere.

I saw the milky way once, at Joshua Tree National Park, not long after Zach died. How can that not be my boy?

I think about him and how amazing it will feel to hug him again, in that mysterious cosmic way.

One day.

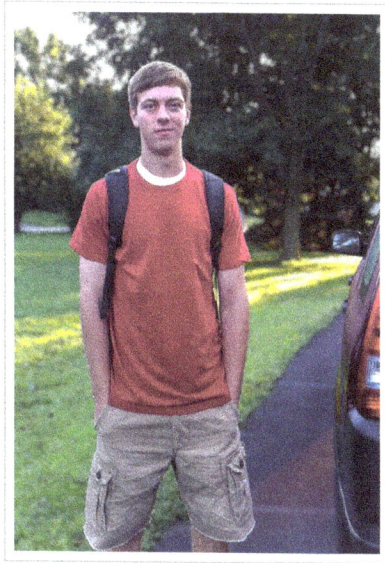

30

Today is the 28th, and it's also twenty-eight months since Zach departed this life.

While this is not the usual smiley pic of Zach, it's the only one with him next to his Honda CRV. It's his first day of junior-year high school. We have five more years ahead in Zach's life.

The other day, I was driving down the highway, and looked in my left-hand mirror. A burgundy Honda CRV was slowly coming up to pass me, this exact car that Zach drove.

I'd not seen his car in a while. That moment—as do many moments—really brought him to mind. I was semi-certain that when it passed me I'd see Zach driving. I can't explain how this one tiny part of me thought it actually would be him. But I at least hoped he'd be a young man, someone who reminded me of Zach (spoiler alert: it was an older Asian man).

It's funny how these kinds of moments, out of the blue, stick with you. Sometimes it can be a sense of melancholy, a fond remembrance that warms the heart. Other times, it can bring the tears spilling over instantly, the sobs from a pain deep within.

Last week was the former, fortunately. I smiled and thought of Zach be-bopping down the road, as the CRV continued on past me. I replayed "car song" memories (thank goodness for the memories that keep Zach very much alive in my heart and mind) and I imagined him driving in whichever way that he's got that wheel now, a way that I can't possibly comprehend.

Drive on, Zach. Drive on...

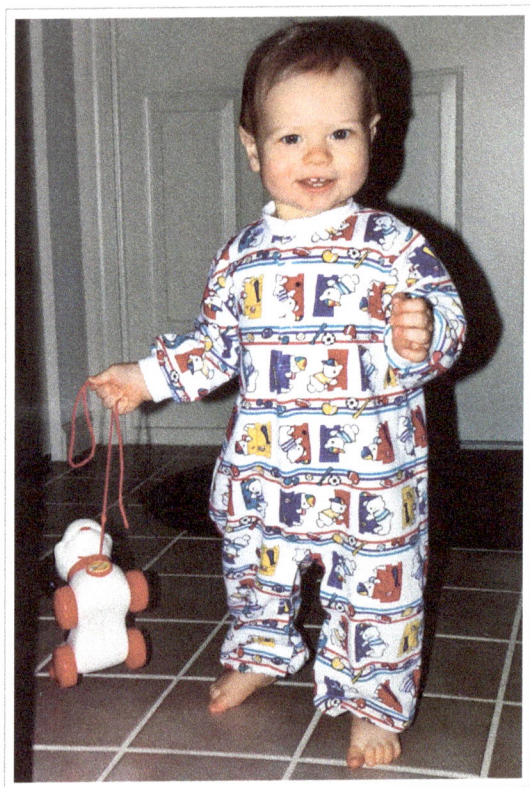

Happy Zach with Snoopy in tow

31

For whatever reason, lately I've been really noticing babies and tod-dlers. They leave me with a strong sense of remembrance of Zach as a baby. It began a bit last night at the Phillies game. They played *Circle of Life* from *The Lion King* while the baseball park videographers panned for people holding up their babies, showing them all on the big ballpark screens. SUPER cute.

Driving home, I had all of these memories come to me, so vivid and present in my mind (and heart), of Zach in a myriad of joyful, play-ful moments, as it goes with babies and toddlers. The laughter and giggles and interaction of just pure love.

And I thought, are you kidding me, life... how can one bring a child into this world, and love them more than anything, and it ends in such a ridiculous, senseless death? How? And why? It's an algo-rithm that clearly went wrong somewhere, somehow.

I have a video of Zach around 18 months old, spinning around and giggling, finally spinning to near his Dad; where his Dad is reach-ing out to poke his belly. And my goodness, it is the cutest thing ever. And I think, where did that joy in Zach's life go? When did the anxiety and the drugs rob that from him? Why can't we tap into that core of giddy happiness that seems almost to disappear once things get messy in life, as one grows into adulthood as an addict?

This ever-complicated brain, with both substance use and mental health disorders, can toss a once-joyful heart almost all out of the window. I just wanted desperately to rein it back in and give it to Zach. Heal his heart and his mind. A HUGE do-over for all of us.

This evening I sat and watched the continuance of summer baby birds and their moms and dads at the bird feeder area out back. It's so sweet to witness them chirping, mouths open, flapping their wings, as they wait to have some food popped into their mouths. Just one more reminder of that circle of life, leaving both a joyful and a heavy heart.

I miss Zach more than any words or feelings I could convey. But then I realize that it's actually quite simple: it's the deepest love I will experience in my life, tucked safely and gently into my heart, forever.

Northern Cardinal

32

Never underestimate the power of nature. Of walking in sunshine, with spring proverbially in the air. Of Zach being in the mix of it as well: that I will never doubt.

All of it, in the end, keeps the heart and mind and soul of a mom whose son has died from completely imploding once and for all. I am grateful for all the beauty I see every day.

And I find it fascinating that I can walk in this newly-birthed season, with joy in my heart, while at the same time holding the hand of grief. How is that possible? I know why I can carry on, even with the loss of Zach still a fresh fifteen months ago today. It's because the joyful parts that come from him will always exist, no matter what thoughts cross my mind, or how much time passes, or how devastating losing him is. Every minute of every day. The profound love I have for him only means that the grief will always be there, hand in hand with the joy.

And it is fifteen months to the day (also a Sunday morning) that my beautiful boy went to sleep and never woke up. Or rather, he woke up to a different place, with "people" who also love him so much—maybe? Helpers on his new journey. And I look outside, tea in hand on this early Sunday morning, and see more of Zach: a bright red cardinal, two blue jays, and even my resident chipmunk, Chip (Zach knew Chip too)!

And so, yup, there is Zach, bringing joy to this day.

Miss you and love you so much Zach, I know you are here in your own special way.

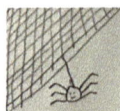

Ex. 3 Pumping Water from a Cylindrical Tank

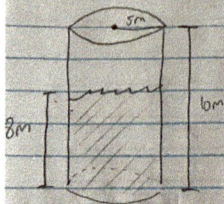

· Density = 9800 N/m³

How much work is required to pump all water to top of tank?

Volume of slice $= \pi r^2 \, dy$
$$= \pi 5^2 \, dy$$
$$= 25\pi \, dy \quad m^3$$

weight of slice $= 9800 \frac{N}{m^2} \cdot 25\pi \, dy \, m^3$

Distance $= 10 - y \, m$

Work $= (9800 \cdot 25\pi) \cdot (10 - y) \, dy$

Work $= \int_0^8 (9800 \cdot 25\pi)(10 - y) \, dy$

3.2

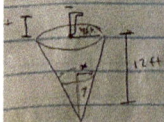

Density $= 62.4 \, lb/ft^3$

Volume of slice $= \pi x^2 \, dy$

$$\frac{x}{y} = \frac{4}{12} \qquad x = \frac{1}{3} y$$

$$\pi \left(\frac{1}{3}y\right)^2 \, dy \quad ft^3$$

Calculus and spiders

118

33

I found a binder with all of Zach's college-level calculus class notes. My first thought: Zach's handwriting was super-small. Fun. Compact and functional, and legible too. I can see him holding a pencil, writing just like this. His penmanship from a young age was excellent: I can recall many grade-school writing assignments in Zach's cursive, where his teachers would comment on how lovely it was.

The second thought on this isn't as warm and fuzzy.

In the couple of years before Zach died, he had convinced himself that he wasn't smart, that his memory was poor. He sometimes would say that it was the air in my house affecting him when he stayed with me. Paranoia is a thing, with drugs. At one point he saw a neurologist, thinking that they could scan his brain and magically tell him what was wrong.

And yet, and yet. Never did he think, or want to hear, the obvious: it was the drugs. IT WAS THE DRUGS.

Imagine as a parent, seeing this decline, this ruining of the body and mind. Because, see, Zach would share with me at times when we talked openly, that he'd tried many, many different drugs. "Everything but heroin" he would say — any or all to alleviate his anxiety. And I would sit there, grateful that he could be honest about this. And I would sit there, the knot twisting in my stomach, and wish that I never ever knew.

This was frustrating, and sad: that he thought so poorly of himself, his self-worth tragically destroyed by the drug use. Drugs altered his brain chemistry, his memory and cognitive function, as well as dinging his whole physical being: this is really what was behind all of it. Sadly, Zach never separated the two: he thought it was always "him."

On top of the drugs was his social anxiety, which also affects memory and learning: another incredibly frustrating fact. As his mom, were it possible I would take it all from him, so that he finally could be free.

In Zach's last fall college semester, his final one, he squeaked by with the highest-level calculus class he would need in order to obtain his Computer Science degree. It was something to be incredibly proud of, for sure, given that he managed schoolwork despite using drugs. I have mad respect for this and oh so many of his other accomplishments.

So: study this document, folks. It's some mad calculus problem from his final. I'm glad he found time for the doodled spider in the corner, too. A happy one, it would seem.

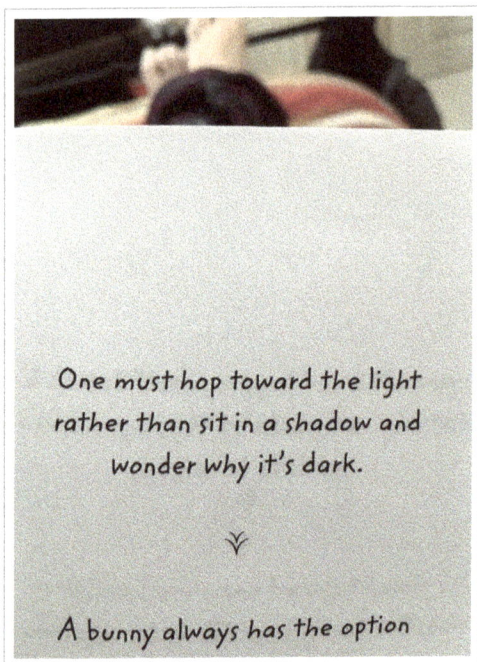

One must hop toward the light rather than sit in a shadow and wonder why it's dark.

❧

A bunny always has the option

Zach reading *Bunny Buddhism*: bonus toes

34

I still have Zach on my cell phone, with our text history back for I'm not sure how long, probably a few years. About a year after his death I read through the most recent ones, a mixture of incredibly difficult and fun texts, along with a few pics he had texted.

One of the texts was in reference to a book I had given Zach called *Bunny Buddhism: Hopping Along the Path to Enlightenment*, the Christmas before he died. It's a cute and inspirational book of little Buddhist philosophical quotes from a bunny's perspective. He sent me this pic he took, which I discovered in the scouring of his texts. I really love his toes at the top, it's what makes the photo. I hadn't remembered this text or pic, so it was a treat to find it.

In addition to the photo, he texted, "I'm hoping the meds will help me 'hop' towards the light I've been absent from for so long." Sigh. Such a simple yet heart-wrenching statement.

Today is the day once again, 23 months since Zach departed this life. So hard to believe. And here, this little photo shows the young man who so much wanted to overcome the challenges that faced him. I sure wish he had been able to do so.

Miss ya, Zach. I know you are in the light all the time now.

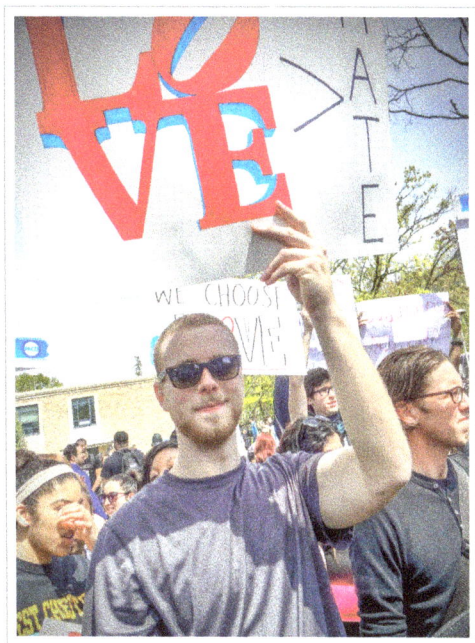

Zach, in the fall of 2016

35

I've been thinking about Zach in all of this disarray in our country, how he's not missing a darned thing, which is one of those silver linings that show themselves often. Of course, I would give anything for him to be here, but the fact that he's not, well, good for you Zach, not having to deal with this shit-show and the stress that comes with it.

There's a bit of irony in this photo, of Zach attending a peaceful protest at a local University with his cousin Kathryn, who made the sign he's holding. This was a protest against the Republican presidential candidate, from when he was campaigning in 2016. I'm proud and happy that Zach was there, given where we were then, and where we are today.

And then, when Zach left us, and we had to decide which photo to display for his memorial service, this was an obvious choice: it is Zach at heart.

Now Zach hangs where I see him most of the day, and he still gives me pause. The constant reminder of the light and love Zach brought to this world at times leaves me speechless.

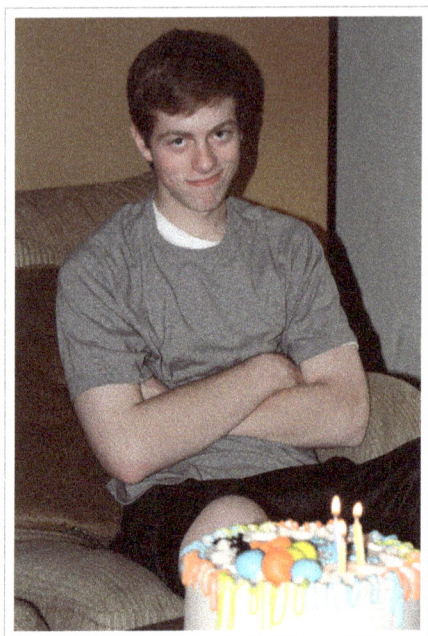

Zach's 17th Birthday

36

April is Zach's birth month. Even after 27 years, I still feel the vibe of 1994 in the air at this time of year, given the almost daily shift in spring blooms and warmish weather. Celebrating Zach's birthday when he is gone from this human life is just another way to keep him alive and remembered. Honored and loved. There's a sense of fervency about it: another moment where I can be sure that Zach is never forgotten.

Remembering keeps me from crumbling.

And Zach loved birthday cake. There will always be cake. We both have quite a sweet tooth: it's no wonder he's my son. Yet another sucky secondary loss: the sweetness of cake and the sweetness of Zach. The boy gone, who should be here, turning 28.

Tomorrow we'll be celebrating together, having Zach's favorite cake, memories shared, and some time in his room at his Dad's place. It too is full of lots of special memorabilia, the perfect sense of Zach Zen.

Happy Cosmic Birthday, Zach! Take a ride by on a shooting star, if you can...

Love Never Leaves

37

When we were searching for an organization to donate to in Zach's memory, it was quickly obvious that the Herren Project was perfect, helping others navigate the road to recovery from the disease of addiction.

Soon after we contacted them, we received a note card, thanking us for naming their organization in Zach's memory. The note card was created by an artist named Becky C, also on the recovery path, and since it moved me so much, I commissioned a piece from her.

Here, the finished result: a beautiful depiction of Zach in the middle of a rainbow spectrum of color, and a just visible *Love Never Leaves* in the bottom yellow band.

I have a friend who has the gift of sensing Zach, and lately he sees him emitting a brilliant light, and a sense of peace. I like pairing that visualization of Zach with this.

Missing you hard Zach, and know you are with us in your sparkly ways.

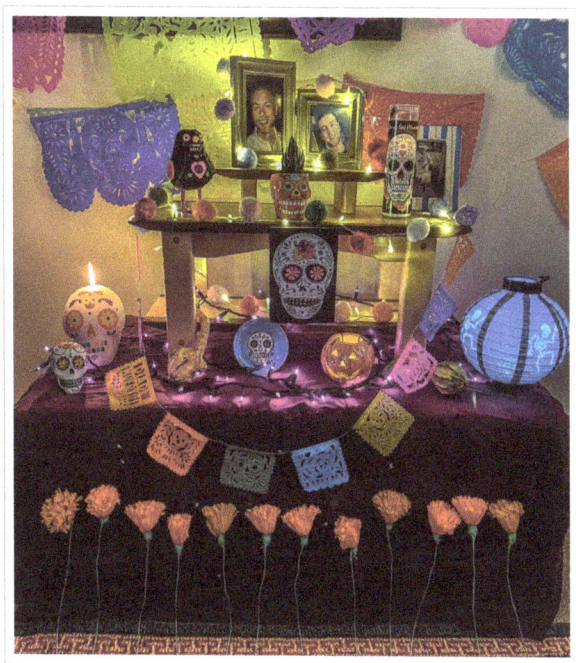

Día de los Muertos Ofrenda (Day of the Dead Altar)

38

Midnight begins *Día de los Muertos*, also known as Day of the Dead: and if you've watched *Coco* (watch it!!!) you'll get the unabridged version of its lovely meaning. Belief has it that the line between the spirit world and the real world dissolves. During this 24-hour period, the souls of the dead return to the living world to feast, drink, dance, and play music with their loved ones. The important thing to know is it's to celebrate, not mourn, while the *ofrenda* (altar) is so the dead know they are not forgotten.

I set up the *ofrenda* with what has become a growing collection of things one might put out: folk-art skeletons and colorful sugar skulls (next year, I will try my hand at actual confectionary sugar skulls), hand-cut paper banners, paper flowers, some knickknacks I found in the Halloween aisle at the Rite Aid, and some hand-crafted keepsakes from Mexico.

Photos, of course! And, FOOD!

Tonight and tomorrow I will add some things that Zach loved: our favorite pizza, an ice-cold root beer, freshly-baked chocolate chip cookies with a tall glass of milk, and some fruit, just in case he wants to pass over the sweets (highly unlikely). Oh, and Halloween candy, of course.

Sure can't wait for your visit, Zach!

Kathryn, Josh, Sam, and Zach: Thanksgiving 2017, Longwood Gardens

39

Zach was the best big cousin. Always loving, sweet, and thoughtful. Being an only child, Zach had his three cousins: all as close to siblings as he would know.

I can watch many videos, look at countless photos of them together, and feel that pang of love and sadness, both. All of them were filled with an ever-loving kindness. None should ever have lost Zach. Such a sad, ridiculous thing for young people to have to carry this in their hearts.

Zach is pictured with his cousins on Thanksgiving Day, his last one with us. I sure do miss him and this crew being together as one. Love abounded; love abounds. One of many favorite lovely and bittersweet memories.

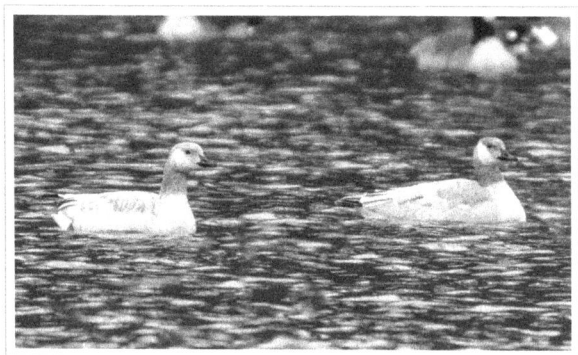

Hi Zach

40

I really love birds; and I find peace, mindfulness, and connection with nature of all kinds, especially as it relates to birds and the power of healing they can bring for me.

Birding has been a passion of mine for over a decade now, as is photography; and it wasn't until Zach died that I found myself in—I guess you could say—a different relationship with birds.

Grieving his loss was a very dark path for some time, and as I slowly found the light again, I discovered something unexpected: birds were revealing themselves to me in a way that ultimately played a part in the healing of my heart.

I now see birds (aside from the beauty and joy they bring) as also offering an amazing gift, in the form of a reminder of Zach, or perhaps a sign from him.

Just a couple weeks ago, early on a wintery Sunday morning, I headed out to a nearby lake where I bird on occasion, and came upon a thousand or so Canada geese. Shortly thereafter, I spotted what looked like two white geese, and immediately pulled my binoculars to my eyes. It was quite a surprise to see a pair of almost angelic-looking Canada geese, both a very diffused white and light gray plumage. And as I took these stunning beauties in, I knew right away these were a gift, a sign. See, the anniversary of Zach's death, which had been heavy on my heart and mind, was coming up in another week.

Once again birds gave me the gift of peace and comfort, the spirit of Zach, and the continued healing of my heart.

Zach

41

Here's a kid who decided one day to take tennis lessons and then made the JV tennis team at his high school, in the spring of his junior year. Zach really had an all-round gift for athleticism, in almost all sports. He wasn't ever looking to be the star player. He just enjoyed sports and the outlet it gave him.

Zach and I would go and hit some tennis balls at a nearby spot. Beautiful courts and off the beaten path: lazy fun, on a cool spring or fall evening. These times really are such an ingrained, solid memory of the many evenings we would stop and hit a few dozen balls, then walk around the court picking them up, in silence. The quiet is something in which we both always shared a similarity. Some people never get it, but we sure knew that talking could be overrated in life.

Today, I will sit in silence, remembering.

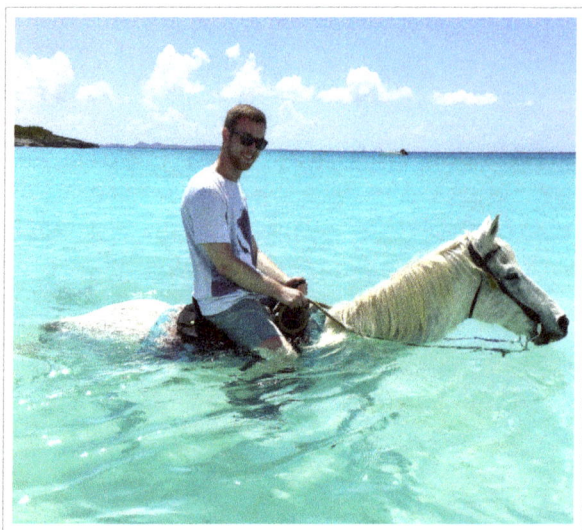

All photos were taken by me:
one of many ways Zach
lives on in my heart

ABOUT THE AUTHOR

Nature explorer, hobbyist photographer, and mindfulness practitioner Liz Pettit is the author of one book (this one!). She finds time daily to be with hope and with as many birds and memories as possible. She has a tiny extended family who mean the world to her, and a snuggly orange tabby cat flat-mate named Luna.